The British Museum

nosy crow

D0833684

THIS
OR
THAT?

Can you spot...

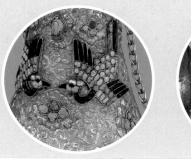

... a lady and her dog?

... a colourful parrot?

... a falcon and a jackal?

... two men wearing yellow?

528 744 45 8

TOGA OR TROUSERS?

All around the world and through history, people have worn different kinds of clothes. What kind of clothes would you like to wear?

Can you see any clothes with flowers on them?

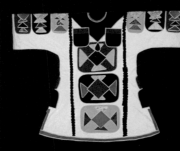

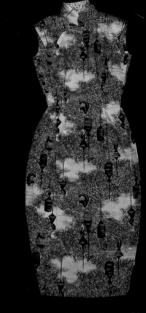
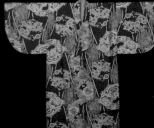

Can you find any stripy trousers?

Can you find a hat with feathers?

BEADS OR BONNET?

All around the world and through history, people have decorated themselves in different ways. Which of these things would you like to wear?

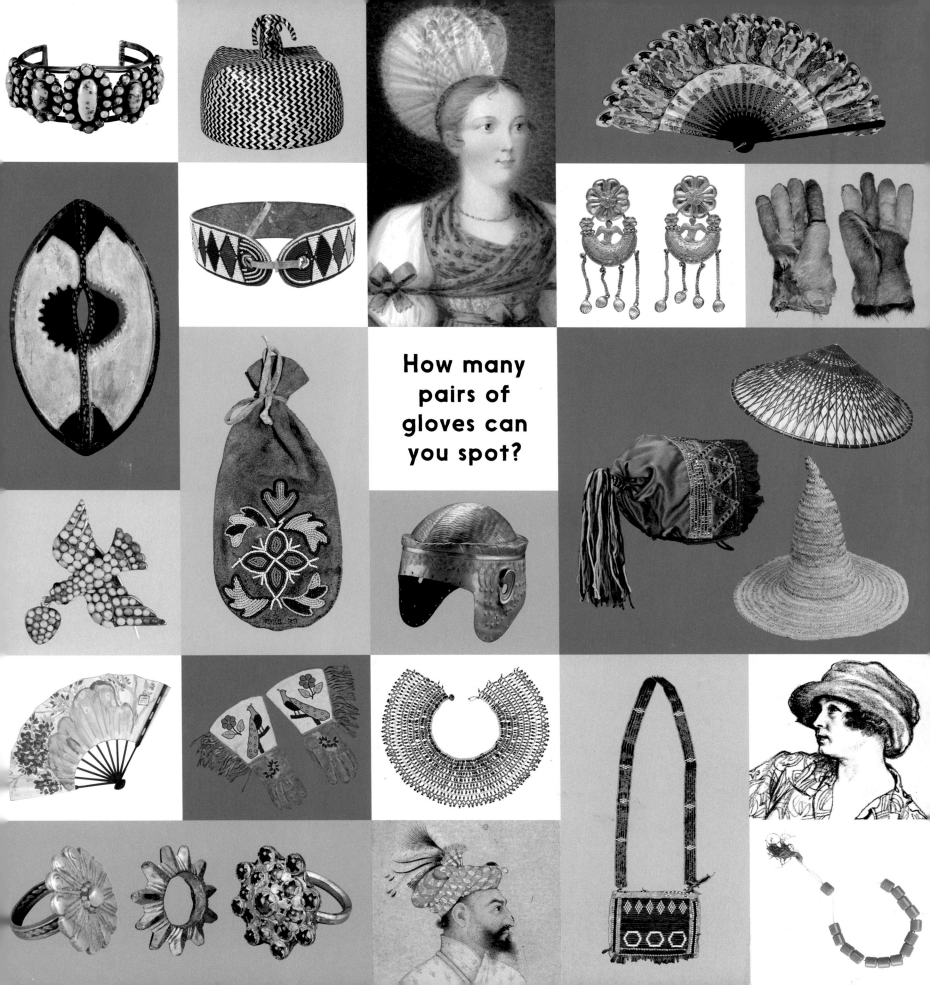

How many
pairs of
gloves can
you spot?

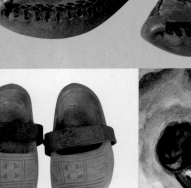

Can you spot a pair of colourful socks?

SANDALS OR SLIPPERS?

All around the world and through history, people have worn different kinds of shoes. Which of these would you like to wear on your feet?

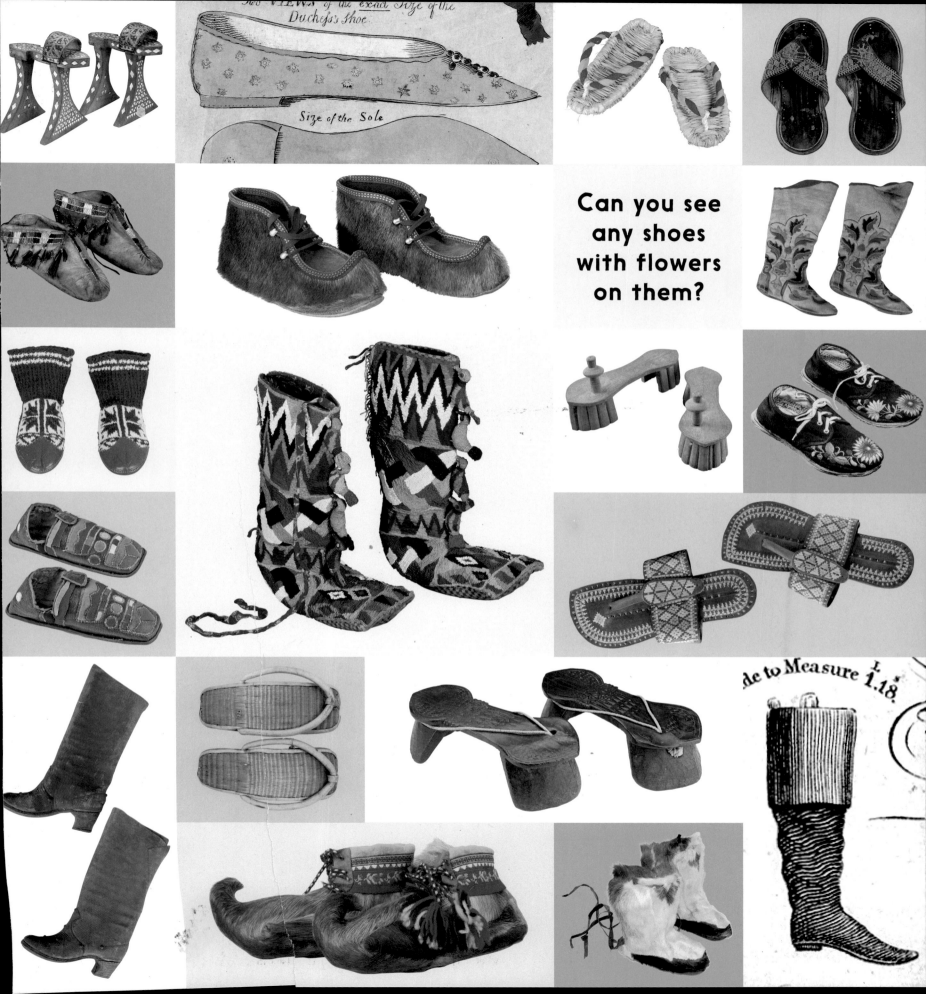

Can you see
any shoes
with flowers
on them?

TENT OR TREEHOUSE?

All around the world and through history, people have built different kinds of buildings. What kind of building would you like to visit?

Can you find any people in the buildings?

Can you see any houses with ladders?

Can you see any objects with horses on?

CLOCK OR CUP?

All around the world and through history, people have had different objects in their homes. Which of these things would you like in your house?

What
would you
use to brush
your hair?

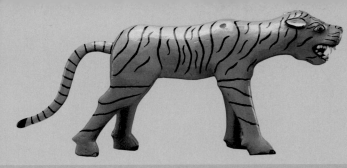

CAMEL
OR CAT?

All around the world and through history,
people and animals have lived side by side.
Which is your favourite animal?

How many animals with stripes can you find?

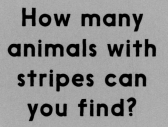

Can you see
an animal
with blue
antlers?

Can you find any creatures that have two heads?

SPHINX OR SERPENT?

All around the world and through history, people have imagined different kinds of mythical beasts. Which one do you like best?

Who is
playing
a pink
guitar?

BOAT OR BALLOON?

All around the world and through history, people have travelled using different kinds of transport. How would you like to get about?

Which vehicles fly through the air?

Can you
find two
elephants?

Can you find any horses with wheels?

DOLL OR DICE?

All around the world and through history,
people have played in different ways.
What kind of toy would you like to play with?

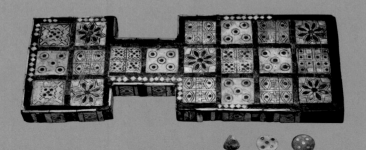

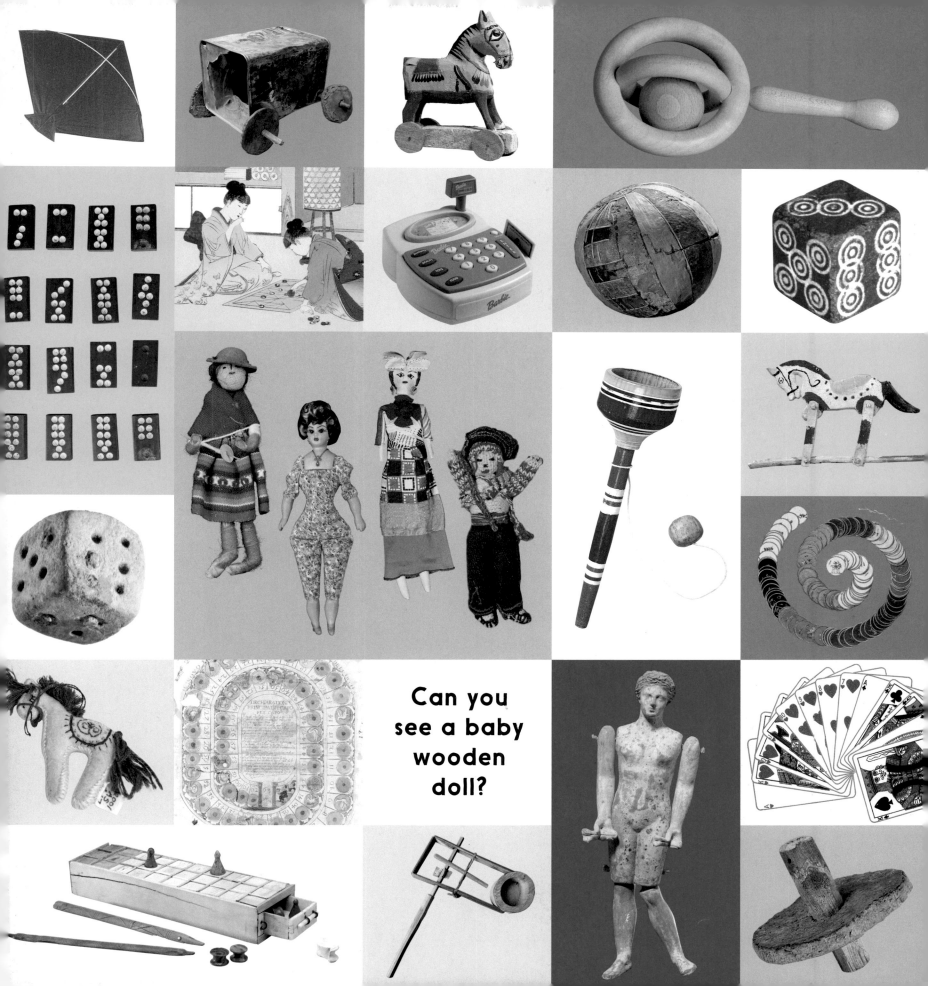

Can you
see a baby
wooden
doll?

HORN OR HARP?

All around the world and through history, people have made different kinds of music. What kind of instrument would you like to play?

Where is the drum with red and white spots?

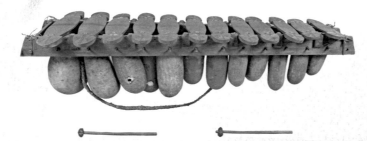

Can you spot a bull's head on an instrument?

Can you see someone cutting a cake?

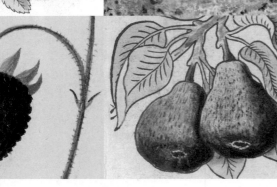

PLUM OR PINEAPPLE?

All around the world and through history, people have eaten different kinds of food. Which of these would you like to eat?

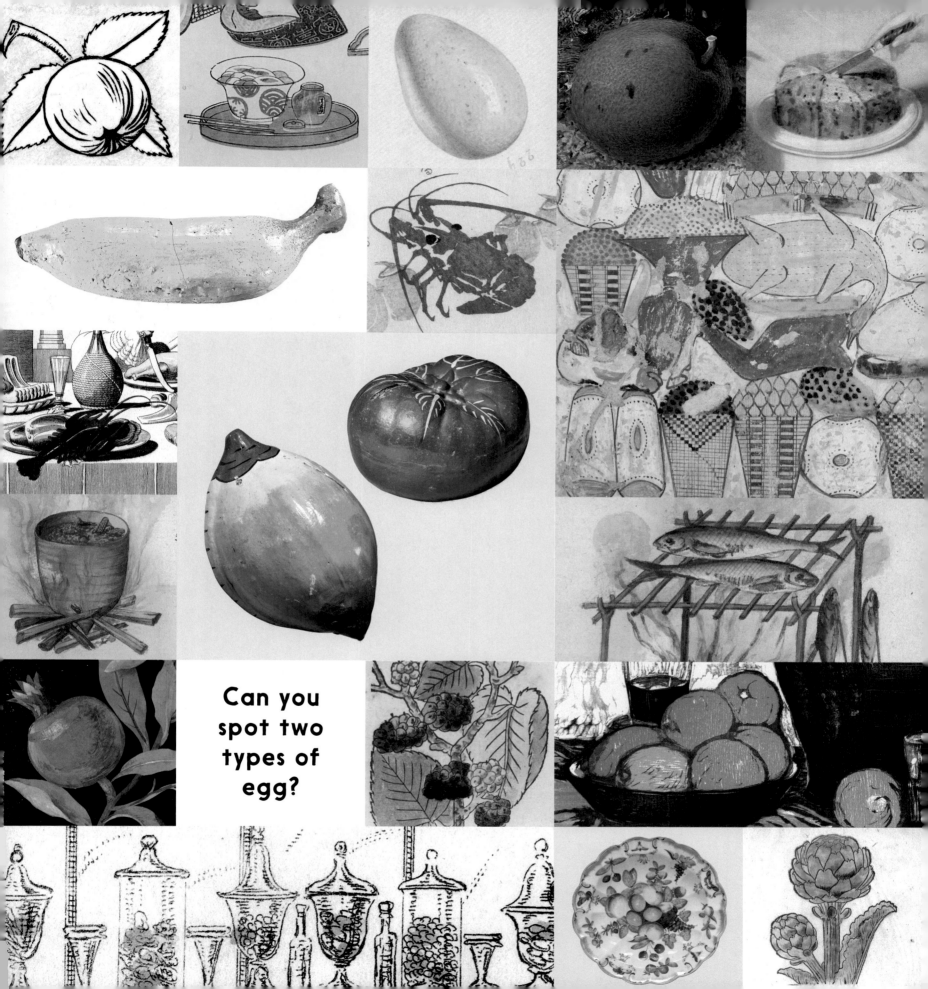

Can you spot two types of egg?

Where is the woman watering a plant?

SOLDIER OR SAILOR?

All around the world and through history, there have been people just like you! Which one of these people would you like to meet?

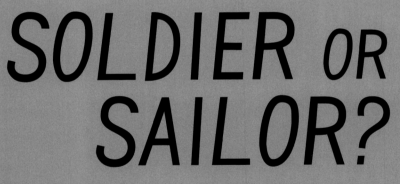

Can you
see anybody
wearing
a hat?

Index

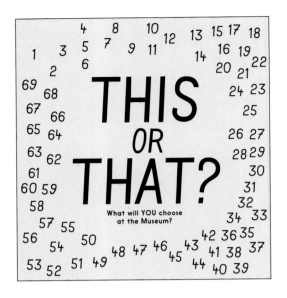

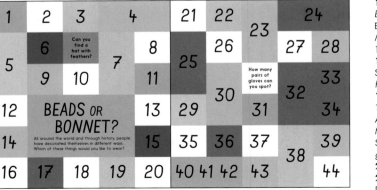

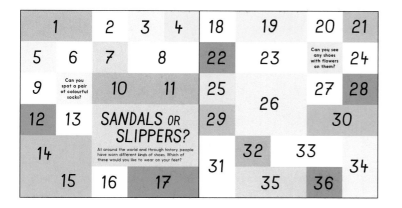

1. *Leather shoes*, Istanbul, Turkey, 1950s–1960s 2. *Etching of girl standing on the ice* by Charles Eduoard Taurel, The Netherlands, 1844–1894 3. *Woollen socks*, Yauli, Peru, Date unknown 4. *Wooden sandals*, Burma, About 1990 5. *Pair of wooden clogs*, Netherlands, 1800–2000 6. *Poster with soldier for shadow puppet theatre*, Greece, 1930–1970 7. *Pair of slippers*, India, About 1990 8. *Wooden shoes*, Korea, 1800–1900 9. *Leather slippers with curled toes*, India, 1800–1900 10. *Pair of leather shoes*, Albania, 1950–2000 11. *Model shoes made from paper*, Penang, Malaysia, 1900–2000 12. *Ink and watercolour portrait of Musa Khan*, Iran, 1651–1750 13. *Wooden shoes with pearl-shell*, India, Probably 1980s 14. *Sandals*, Burma, About 1880 15. *Ceramic shoes*, Kirman, Iran, 1600–1650 16. *Goat-skin shoes*, Kano, Nigeria, 1970–1974 17. *Jingly clogs*, Aleppo, Syria, 1800–1900 18. *Wooden bath clogs*, Turkey, 1800–1850 19. *Hand-coloured etching titled 'The Duchess blush or York Flame'* by Isaac Cruikshank, UK, 1791 20. *Rice-straw sandals*, Hinokage, Japan, 1987 21. *Leather sandals*, Wodaabe people, Niger, About 2004 22. *Leather moccasins*, North America, Date unknown 23. *Pair of reindeer-skin boots*, Norway, 1959 24. *Embroidered leather boots*, Kazakhstan, 1900–1950 25. *Knitted slippers*, Bosnia, 1900–1950 26. *Beaded boots*, Yoruba people, Nigeria, About 1900–1903 27. *Wooden sandals*, Zanzibar, 1920–1927 28. *Pair of cotton shoes*, Sichuan, China, 1990s 29. *Leather slippers with wool applique*, Berber people, Morocco, About 1969 30. *Goat-skin sandals*, Somalia, About 1900–1928 31. *Leather boots*, Kazakhstan, 1800–1900 32. *Slippers made of bamboo and leather*, Japan, Before 1753 33. *Wooden shoes*, Afghanistan, 1900–1950 34. *Dickens, boot and shoemaker's trade card* by Folkard, UK, Date unknown 35. *Reindeer skin boots*, Finland, 1975 36. *Reindeer and seal boots*, Russia, 1990s

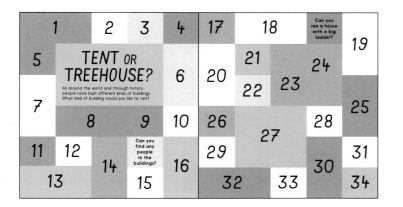

1. *Watercolour drawing of a house* by John Bewick, UK, 1760–1795 2. *Brass model of a house*, Sumatra, Indonesia, About 1900 3. *Watercolour painting of the Taj Mahal*, India, 1800–1850 4. *Bamboo model house*, Nicobar Islands, India, About 1900 5. *Bamboo model hut*, Nicobar Islands, India, About 1900 6. *Watercolour drawing of a house* by Frederick Nash, UK, 1800–1817 7. *Watercolour of a tree house*, Papua New Guinea, 1900–1950 8. *Gouache painting of Rama and Sita*, India, 1790–1810 9. *Watercolour drawing of a house* by Robert Dixon, UK, 1780–1815 10. *Porcelain water-dropper in the shape of a house*, Korea, 2000 11. *Woodcut of a mosque* by Melchior Lorck, Germany, 1570 12. *Netsuke palace* by Kagetoshi, Japan, 1800–1850 13. *Watercolour drawing of Harewood House* by Thomas Sandby, UK, 1738–1798 14. *Wooden model house*, Nicobar Islands, India, About 1900 15. *Wood-engraving of a country house* by Thomas Bewick, UK, 1778–1828 16. *Hand-coloured aqua-tint titled 'The Light-house on Point of Air, Flintshire'* by William Daniell, UK, 1815 17. *Photograph of thatched house*, Samoa, Polynesia, 1880 18. *Woodblock print of houseboat* by Shibata Zeshin, Japan, 1847 or 1859 19. *Sandstone model of temple*, India, 1700–1900 20. *Model rice field house*, Java, Indonesia, 1830–1860s 21. *Etching titled 'The Mad King's Castle'* by Percival Gaskell, UK, 1883–1913 22. *Painting of 'The month of Bhadrapada or Badon'*, Amber, India, 1700–1725 23. *Model house* by John Gwaytihl, Masset, Canada, 1890s 24. *Model rest house*, Burma, 1870s–1880s 25. *Woodblock print of the lighthouse at Tempozan Park* by Shumpo, Japan, 1879 26. *Wood-engraving of a winter scene* by Thomas Bewick, UK, 1791–1797 27. *Watercolour drawing of a house design* by Thomas Sandby, UK, 1738–1798 28. *Palm leaf, wood and barkcloth model house*, Samoa, About 1850 29. *Watercolour drawing of a windmill* by Arthur James Stark, UK, 1831–1902 30. *Ceramic house* by Omar Mahdaoui, Palestine, 1900–2000 31. *Wooden model house*, Singapore, About 1800–2000 32. *Watercolour drawing of Vine Cottage* by Thomas Hosmer Shepherd, UK, 1793–1864 33. *Etching of a landscape* by Francis Vivares, UK, 1739 34. *Photograph of a lighthouse platform* by JM Booth, Brisbane, Australia, 1930s

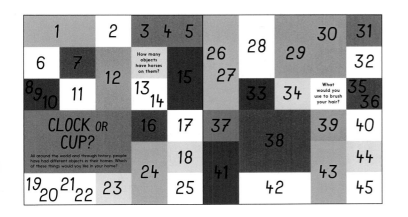

1. *Wooden sewing machine table*, Turkmenistan, 1980–1990s 2. *Birch bark cushion*, Finland, 2000–2010 3. *Porcelain teapot*, Worcester, UK, 1751–1783 4. *Porcelain teapot*, China, 1662–1722 5. *Metal teapot*, Ladakh, India, 1977 6. *Copper oil lamp*, Sudi, Nepal, About 1980s 7. *Low straight-backed chair*, Thebes, Egypt, About 1550–1295 BC 8. *Wooden fork*, Somalia, About 1940–1970 9. *Wooden spoon*, Urumqi, China, 1900s 10. *Silver fish knife*, Dusseldorf, Germany, 1916–1917 11. *Wooden basket*, Yuncheng, China, Date unknown 12. *Oak longcase clock*, Huddersfield, UK, 1775–1785 13. *Horn comb*, Scotland, 1900–1950 14. *Oval hair brush* by Oomersee Mawjee, Bhuj, India, 1900–1950 15. *Porcelain vase*, China, 1800–1900 16. *Porcelain bowl*, China, 1723–1735 17. *Wood-engraving of a bookcase* by Thomas Bewick, UK, 1782–1783 18. *Lacquered wood table*, Japan, 1800–1900 19. *Goblet*, Gateshead, UK, About 1880 20. *Bamboo and lacquer tumbler*, Burma, 1910–1920s 21. *Water vessel*, Somalia, 1900–1930 22. *Goblet*, Egypt, 1077–943 BC 23. *Silver mirror*, Place unknown, Date unknown 24. *Navajo woven wool blanket*, USA, 1860 25. *Woven food basket*, South Africa, 1980–1991 26. *Bamboo model of a ladder*, Andaman Islands, India, 1850–1900 27. *Wooden broom*, Japan, Date unknown 28. *Wooden chair*, Zambia, About 1900–1940 29. *Cloisonne jar*, China, 1426–1435 30. *Black-figured amphora* by The Lysippides Painter, Greece, 520–500 BC 31. *Watercolour drawing* by John Wykeham Archer, Pre-1874 32. *Model stool made of wood*, China, 1800–1900 33. *Porcelain sugar box*, Meissen, Germany, About 1730 34. *Silk cushion cover*, Lebanon, 1980s 35. *Key-shaped pilgrim badge*, Italy, About AD 400–1500 36. *Key*, Maldives, 1900–1980 37. *Model cradle*, Armenia, 1900–1950 38. *Hand-coloured lithograph of the Queen's bedroom*, UK, 1840 39. *Striking clock*, UK, 1920–1928 40. *Casket*, Limoges, France, About 1180 41. *Porcelain fish vase*, China, 1662–1722 42. *Woven war rug*, Afghanistan, 1979–1989 43. *Oval mirror* by Oomersee Mawjee, Bhuj, India, 1900–2000 44. *Porcelain jug*, Worcester, UK, Date unknown 45. *Wooden stool with beaded seat*, Kenya, Late 1900s or early 2000s

CAT OR CAMEL?

All around the world and through history, people have lived with animals around them. Which one is your favourite animal?

How many animals with stripes can you find?

Can you see an animal with blue antlers?

1. *Pottery camel*, Probably Somalia, 1930s **2.** *Porcelain swan*, Lowestoft, UK, About 1780 **3.** *Wooden tiger figure*, Mexico, 1980s **4.** *Pottery horse figure*, Dinajour, Bangladesh, Date unknown **5.** *Ink sketch of crab*, Japan, 1800–1900 **6.** *Etching of a giraffe* by Samuel Howitt, UK, 1812 **7.** *Pottery dog*, Pernambuco, Brazil, Mid 1900s **8.** *Pottery crocodile*, Jalisco, Mexico, 1970s **9.** *Toy snake figure*, Tlaquepaque, Mexico, 1970s **10.** *Porcelain elephant*, Japan, 1655–1670 **11.** *Toy zebra* by Kay Bojesen, Denmark, 1935 **12.** *Glazed hippopotamus*, Egypt, 2000–1700 BC **13.** *Woodblock print of a kingfisher* by Chikuseki, Japan, About 1900 **14.** *Terracotta horse figure*, Boeotia, Greece, 580–550 BC **15.** *Pottery lion toy*, Palugama, Sri Lanka, 1980s **16.** *Model lizard*, Bangkok, Thailand, 1880–1906 **17.** *Gold brooch in the form of a poodle*, France, About 1900–1950 **18.** *Pottery fish figure*, Dhaka, Bangladesh, 1900–1980s **19.** *Fish amulet*, Ur, Iraq, 2600 BC **20.** *Painted porcelain plaque* by Sampson Hancock, Derby, UK, About 1830 **21.** *Bronze bull figure*, Egypt, About 400–300 BC **22.** *Toy dog* by Kay Bojesen, Denmark, 1934 **23.** *Watercolour of a bird* by Nicolas Robert, France, 1625–1684 **24.** *Dove-shaped wooden badge*, UK, 1980s **25.** *'The Gazi Scroll' Bengal*, India, About 1800 **26.** *Blue glazed cat*, Egypt, AD 100 **27.** *Pottery cat*, Palugama, Sri Lanka, 1900–1980s **28.** *Papercut of fish*, China, 1986 **29.** *Gold and enamel camel figure*, Jaipur, India, 1850s–1860s **30.** *Glass vessel*, Egypt, 18th dynasty **31.** *Watercolour drawing of a bird* by Nicholas Robert, France, 1625–1684 **32.** *Clay frog figure*, India, About 1980 **33.** *Watercolour painting of a penguin* by John Webber, UK, 1777 **34.** *Etching titled 'True portrait of the she-antbear'* by Andres de le Muela, Spain, 1776 **35.** *Gold llama figure*, Peru, About 1500 **36.** *Porcelain cat*, Jingdezhen, China, 1690–1722 **37.** *Gold and enamel deer figure*, Jaipur, India, 1850s–1860s **38.** *Wooden grasshopper figurine*, San Antonia Arrazola, Mexico, 1980s **39.** *Polar bear figure* by Aibilie Innuksuk, Igloolik Island, Canada, 1986

SPHINX OR SERPENT?

All around the world and through history, people have imagined different kinds of mythical beasts. Which one do you like best?

Can you find two creatures that have two heads?

Who is playing a pink guitar?

1. *Wood-engraving of winged dragon* by Thomas Bewick, UK, 1778–1790 **2.** *Papercut of a dragon*, Yangzhou, China, 1985–1995 **3.** *Articulated iron dragon* by Myochin Kiyohara, Japan, 1700–1900 **4.** *Porcelain dish with dragon*, China, 1662–1722 **5.** *Woodblock print 'Newly published collection of masks'* by Utatora, Japan, 1863 **6.** *Glazed dragon ewer*, Vietnam, 1450–1480 **7.** *Porcelain dragon vase*, China, 1700–1800 **8.** *Ivory panel showing sphinx*, Iraq, 900–700 BC **9.** *Unicorn standing cup*, Nuremberg, Germany, 1579–1605 (head and base), 1800–1898 (body and shields) **10.** *Gouache painting of phoenix and dragon*, India, 1800–1900 **11.** *Wooden tiger figure*, Dhaka, Bangladesh, 1980s **12.** *Silver coin*, Syracuse, Italy, 400–300 BC **13.** *Earthenware tile* by William de Morgan, Fulham, UK, 1898–1907 **14.** *Skeleton Ox*, Ocotlán de Morelos, Mexico, 1970s **15.** *Wooden animal figure*, Nicobar Islands, India, Date unknown **16.** *The Pegasus Vase*, UK, 1786 **17.** *Woodblock print 'Newly published collection of masks'* by Utatora, Japan, 1863 **18.** *Power figure*, Bakongo people, Democratic Republic of Congo, About 1875–1905 **19.** *Woodblock print 'Newly published collection of masks'* by Utatora, Japan, 1863 **20.** *Papier-mâché figurine*, Tlalpujahua, Mexico, 1980s **21.** *Woodblock print of storm dragon* by Totoya Hokkei, Japan, 1820s–1830s **22.** *Papier-mâché dragon figure*, Tlalpujahua, Mexico, 1980s **23.** *Woodcut of a griffin* by Heinrich Petri, Basel, Switzerland, 1544–1552 **24.** *Earthenware glazed tile*, China, 1366–1400 **25.** *Gold plaque ornament from the Oxus Treasure*, Tajikistan, 600–500 BC **26.** *Silver bowl cover*, Mildenhall, UK, AD 300–400 **27.** *Papier-mâché dragon figure*, Mexico City, Mexico, 1992 **28.** *Double-headed serpent mosaic*, Mexico, 1400–1521 **29.** *Pair of porcelain lion-dogs*, Jingdezhen, China, 1662–1722 **30.** *Pottery mermaid figurine*, Metepec, Mexico, 1980s **31.** *Ogre shadow puppet*, Tumpat, Malaysia, About 1950 **32.** *Pegasus cast bronze medal* by Gottfried Schadow, Germany, 1815 **33.** *Linocut of a phoenix* by Henry Keen, UK, 1925–1930

BOAT OR BALLOON?

All around the world and through history, people have used different kinds of transport. How would you like to get about?

Can you find two elephants?

Which four vehicles travel through the air?

1. *Toy bus made of tin*, Palugama, Sri Lanka, 1980s **2.** *Gouache painting of Krishna*, India, 1790–1810 **3.** *Model boat*, Chennai, India, 1800–1900 **4.** *Part of a panel from a mosaic pavement*, Halicarnassus, Turkey, AD 300–400 **5.** *Model bullock cart*, India, 1800–1900 **6.** *Model canoe*, Malakula, Vanuatu, Date unknown **7.** *Wooden model cart*, Sri Lanka, About 1850 **8.** *Steam train illustration* by Perkins & Heath, UK, 1829–1835 **9.** *Toy lorry*, Miakara, Madagascar, Early 1980s **10.** *Plaited bicycle figurine*, Chigmecatitlan, Mexico, 1970s **11.** *Wood-engraving of a ship* by Thomas Bewick, UK, 1779 **12.** *Model chariot*, Tajikistan, 500–301 BC **13.** *Ink drawing of a boat*, China, 1820 **14.** *Model motor car*, Bangkok, Thailand, Date unknown **15.** *Gouache painting of man riding a camel*, India, 1800–1850 **16.** *Etching titled 'How to ride with Elegance thro' the Streets'* by James Gillray, UK, 1800 **17.** *Funerary equipment in the form of a model motor car*, Penang, Malaysia, 1980s **18.** *Woodblock print of a Dutch ship*, Japan, 1800–1850 **19.** *Wooden model aeroplane*, Madagascar, 1980–1985 **20.** *Toy helicopter*, Vatomasy, Madagascar, Early 1980s **21.** *Figurine of skeleton man and cart*, Puebla, Mexico, 1980s **22.** *Cycle rickshaw*, Dhaka, Bangladesh, 1980s **23.** *Aluminium toy bicycle*, Delhi, India, 1991 **24.** *Drawing of a procession of the King of Kabul*, India, About 1840 **25.** *Wood-engraving of man riding wagon* by William Dickes, UK, 1830–1892 **26.** *Etching titled 'View of the ascent of Mr Lunardi's Celebrated air Balloon from the Artillery Ground Sept. 15th 1784'* by Thomas Deeble, UK, 1784 **27.** *Toy motorbike*, Papantla, Mexico, 1980s **28.** *Woodblock print* by Kawabata Gyokusho, Japan, 1880–1886 **29.** *Model motor bus*, Mexico City, Mexico, 1980s **30.** *Model aeroplane*, Yucatan, Mexico, 1970s **31.** *Funerary equipment in the form of a model motor bicycle*, Penang, Malaysia, 1980s **32.** *Boat model*, Probably Indonesia, Probably 1800s **33.** *Wooden figure of a policeman riding a bicycle*, Kenya, Before 1982 **34.** *Watercolour drawing of a coastal scene* by Theodore Gudin, France, 1817–1880

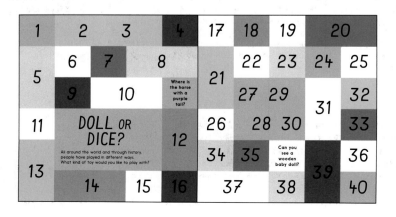

DOLL OR DICE?

All around the world and through history, people have played in different ways. What kind of toy would you like to play with?

Where is the horse with a purple tail?

Can you see a wooden baby doll?

1. *Three wooden kokeshi dolls*, Sendai City, Japan, Probably 1900–2000 **2.** *The Lewis Chessmen*, Uig, Scotland, 1150–1175 **3.** *Wooden cat figure*, Thebes, Egypt, About 1550–1069 BC **4.** *Spinning top*, Ritabel, Indonesia, 1800–1900 **5.** *Paper kite*, Cuetzalan del Progreso, Mexico, 1980s **6.** *Wooden toy horse on wheels*, Akhmim, Egypt, About AD 1–300 **7.** *Toy basket*, Dhaka, Bangladesh, 1980s **8.** *Game box, counters and dice*, Dhaka, Bangladesh, 1980s **9.** *Rattan ball*, Malaysia, 1950s **10.** *Toy clay mouse*, Egypt, 1550–1070 BC **11.** *Pottery game-pieces*, Egypt, About 1550–343 BC **12.** *Toy catapult*, Vezo people, Madagascar, Early 1980s **13.** *Part of a game made of shell*, Johor, Malaysia, 1880s–1910 **14.** *The Royal Game of Ur*, Iraq, 2600 BC **15.** *Plastic toy oxen*, Dhaka, Bangladesh, 1980s **16.** *Toy made of paper and wood*, Dhaka, Bangladesh, 1980s **17.** *Kite*, Ahmedabad, India, 1950s–1980s **18.** *Toy car*, Ladakh, India, 1977 **19.** *Toy horse with wheels*, Dhamrai, Bangladesh, 1900–1980s **20.** *Wooden rattle* by Kay Bojesen, Denmark, 1932 **21.** *Set of dominoes*, Burma, About 1850s–1880s **22.** *Woodblock print of children playing a game* by Miyagawa Shuntei, Japan, 1896 **23.** *Toy cash register*, China, 2003 **24.** *Linen toy ball*, Egypt, 30 BC–AD 641 **25.** *Stone dice*, Location unknown, Date unknown **26.** *Sandstone dice*, Egypt, 700–600 BC **27.** *Doll made of acrylic yarn and wire*, Lake Titicaca, South America, 1990s **28.** *Doll made of wax and textile*, Puebla, Mexico, 1980s **29.** *Doll made of cloth*, Cajamarca, Peru, Date unknown **30.** *Doll*, Huancavelica, Peru, Date unknown **31.** *Wooden toy*, San Antonio de la Isla, Mexico, 1970s **32.** *Wooden toy horse*, Mexico, 1970s **33.** *Playing cards*, Orissa, India, 1950s